Lemonade

and Other Poems Squeezed from a Single Word

by Bob Raczka

Illustrated by
Nancy Doniger

SQUARE
FISH

Roaring Brook Press
New York

SQUARE
FISH

An Imprint of Macmillan

"rain" first published in i to iran (IZEN, 1990)
used with the permission of Andrew Russ

Library of Congress Cataloging-in-Publication Data
Raczka, Bob
Lemonade, and other poems squeezed from a single world / Bob Raczka;
illustrations by Nancy Doniger.
p. cm.
ISBN 978-1-250-01894-6
1. Children's poetry, American.--I. Doniger, Nancy, ill.--II. Title.

PS3618.A346L46 2010   811'.6--dc22   2010024807

Originally published in the United States by Roaring Brook Press
First Square Fish Edition: March 2013
Square Fish logo designed by Filomena Tuosto
mackids.com

2 4 6 8 10 9 7 5 3 1

CONTENTS

I love playing with words. That's why I write poems.

I also love to see how other people play with words. That's why I read poems.

One day I was reading about poems on the Internet, and I came across the poetry of Andrew Russ. Andrew makes poems out of single words. Here's my favorite:

rain

i
ra n
in

As you can see, Andrew used "rain" as his title, and then he wrote three more words using only the letters from the word "rain."

And what a poem! In just three short words, in just six letters, Andrew has captured how rain makes us feel.

You probably noticed that the letters in Andrew's poem are oddly spaced. That's because he lined up each letter in his poem under the same letter in his title. This not only makes his poem more interesting to look at, it proves that he is sticking to his rule of using only the letters in his title word.

After I discovered one-word poems, I just had to try writing some for myself. I hope you enjoy them and even try to write your own.

Bob

lemonade

    m ade
     on e
      ad

     ad
      de
      d

    on e
   lemon
  l o ad

     a
    n d

   on e

   mo
  m

lemonade

made
one
ad

added
one
lemon
load

and
one
mom

bleachers

b   a
l
l

        r
       e
ache s

      her
       e

b   a   s
      e s

     c
lea   r

    che
     ers

<u>bleachers</u>

ball
reaches
here

bases
clear

cheers

```
          moonlight

                  h
      o           t

      n ight

                  t
                  h
          i
      n

          light

      mo          t
                  h

          i
      n

      mo          t
          i
      on
```

moonlight

hot
night

thin
light

moth
in
motion

treehouse

```
              ou
          r
                  s
              ho
          re
              h   u
          t
              ou
          r
                  s
              ho    e
                  s
          t       o
          re
              ou
          r
              h     e
          r   o
                  s
          r   o
              o  s
          t
```

treehouse

our
shore
hut

our
shoe
store

our
heroes
roost

```
vacation

   ac  tion
          i  n
       a
   va      n
```

<u>vacation</u>

action
in
a
van

constellation

a

s   i

l

e

n t

l ion

tell

s

a   n

a

n

c   i

e

n t

t

a

l

e

constellation

a
silent
lion
tells
an
ancient
tale

```
breakfast

        a f    t
     e
     r

     re        st

        ea      t
           fast
                as
           a
     b  ea    st
```

13

breakfast

after
rest

eat
fast
as
a
beast

friends

fr e d
f i nds
  e d

<u>friend</u>

fred
finds
ed

playground

```
        r un
    a    round
    a      nd
play
    l    ou d
    la     nd
```

playground

run
around
and
play
loud
land

ladybug

  a

     bug

       g

    y

     bu

  d

  dy

  a

      g

lad

      g

  a

 l

ladybug

a
buggy
buddy

a
glad
gal

minivan

ivan

in

a
va

in

i an

in

mi   a

in

n an

in

an
n
a

in

minivan

ivan
in

ava
in

ian
in

mia
in

nan
in

anna
in

halloween

  all

  al o   n
          e

   a   n

    ow
   l

   a

 h ow
   l
    o
 h
        n

   o

23

halloween

all
alone

an
owl

a
howl

oh
no

spaghetti

pa
pa

      h
   a
s

   a

pa
s   t
 a

  a
p
p   et i
       t
    e

   he
      e
 a   t
s

   he
  a
p
s

spaghetti

papa
has
a
pasta
appetite

he
eats
heaps

creative

       i

   cr a ve

     a

  r t

creative

i
crave
art

snowflakes

          a

      f   e

     w

     flakes

     f a

      l

      l

      a

   n   e

    w

      s

      e

      a

  s o

   n

     a

   w akes

<u>snowflakes</u>

a
few
flakes
fall

a
new
season
awakes

```
        chocolate

    h      at

        co  at

    h  o  t
  c  oco  a
```

chocolate

hat

coat

hot
cocoa

television
        s
      e
    t

      is

        on
          i
            s
            i
    t

<u>television</u>

set
is
on

i
sit

```
pepperoni

          on
        e

      p       i
        e

            n
        o


   pepper

            n
          o

          oni
          on
```

pepperoni

one
pie

no
pepper

no
onion

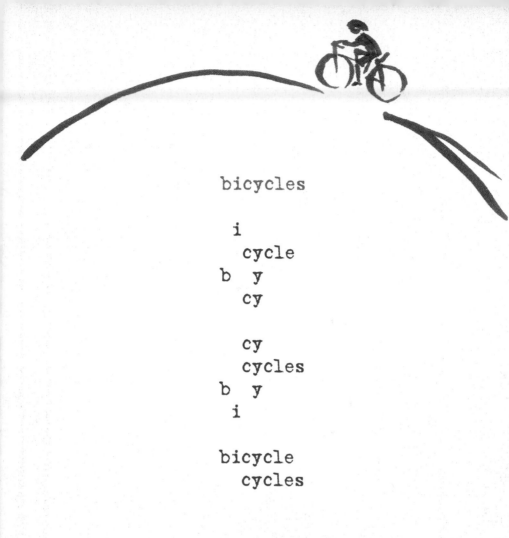

```
    bicycles

    i
      cycle
  b   y
      cy

        cy
      cycles
  b   y
    i

    bicycle
      cycles
```

bicycles

i
cycle
by
cy

cy
cycles
by
i

bicycle
cycles

earthworms

   a

             s

       h or

   t

             s

   t orm

     worms

       h

  e r

  e

     worms

     th

  e r

  e

       w

  ear

          s

     h o   s

  e   s

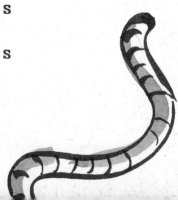

earthworms

a
short
storm

worms
here

worms
there

wear
shoes

spring

    i

s   ing

    i

sp in

    i

      g

rin

spring

i
sing

i
spin

i
grin

flowers

    we

        s

   low

  f o   r

  f   r

       e

      e

    w

  ow s

43

flowers

we
slow
for
free
wows